The Flower of Youth

The Flower of Youth

Pier Paolo Pasolini Poems

Mary di Michele

MISFIT
ECW Press

Published by ECW Press
2120 Queen Street East, Suite 200, Toronto, Ontario, Canada M4E 1E2
416-694-3348 / info@ecwpress.com

Library and Archives Canada Cataloguing in Publication

Di Michele, Mary, 1949-
The flower of youth : Pier Paolo Pasolini poems / Mary di Michele.

ISBN 978-1-77041-048-0
Also issued as: 978-1-77090-107-0 (PDF); 978-1-77090-106-3 (ePUB)

1. Pasolini, Pier Paolo, 1922-1975—Poetry. I. Title.

PS8557.I55F66 2011 C811'.54 C2011-902944-8

Editor for the press: Michael Holmes / a misFit book
Cover and text design: Tania Craan
Cover photo: "Basilica in the Mist," 1957, courtesy Elio Ciol
Typesetting: Mary Bowness
Printing: Coach House Printing 1 2 3 4 5

The publication of *The Flower of Youth* has been generously supported by the Canada Council for the Arts, which last year invested $20.1 million in writing and publishing throughout Canada, by the Ontario Arts Council, by the Government of Ontario through Ontario Book Publishing Tax Credit, by the OMDC Book Fund, an initiative of the Ontario Media Development Corporation, and by the Government of Canada through the Canada Book Fund.

Canada Council for the Arts / Conseil des Arts du Canada
Canada
ONTARIO ARTS COUNCIL
CONSEIL DES ARTS DE L'ONTARIO

PRINTED AND BOUND IN CANADA

. . . sed carmina tantum
nostra ualent, Lycida, tela inter Martia quantum
Chaonias dicunt Aquila uneniente columbas.

Virgil, Ecloga IX

. . . but what can poetry do
against marching armies? When the eagle flies
tell me what good is the crooning of doves?

contents

I

Prologue:
The Flower and the Book

Vietato (A Town Called Forbidden)

After the hum of the transatlantic jet
the earthbound jerk and rattle of a train
pulling in and out of small town stations
en route Venezia — Udine —
there's the heat of the sun high
in a May sky, there's the haze
of humidity or my sleepless eyes
see now as if submerged
underwater, I understand
nothing, not the time of day,
not the names of towns:
Salice, Pordenone, Vietato —
Vietato, not the name of a town at all,
but a warning sign, *Forbidden* —
as if this flat and sun-lit terrain could take me
back to the prairie, to Saskatchewan,
where a town called Forbidden
might join one called Forget.

I was bound for Beyond History, a conference at the university in Udine but later I hoped to find a village called Casarsa though I had no idea how to get there, so when I saw Casarsa delle Delizia as one of the stops printed on my train ticket, it felt like a gift. The first of many I was to receive.

•

A beautiful day, full sun, breezes making it feel almost cool, although how can it be cool at 28°C? I'm now staying at a hotel in Casarsa called Al Posta; it's near the post office. I take tea in the garden, at a table shaded by a tree. I breathe deeply and the air smells green and tastes almost sweet. I listen.

Your music,
oleander and mosquito,
muted in May.

I would lose the latter part of that duet.

Ah, but what is it if
it cannot pierce, if
it cannot get under your skin?

I hear him whispering,
"Such music's emasculated."

Quietus

(*campo santo*, Casarsa, Italia)
(Pier Paolo Pasolini 1922–75)

Row upon row of headstones, there's no green, no grass, just dust and gravel paths around the graves. I walk among them looking for him. Photos of the dead mark most of the graves — their faces, their presence absence. They seem to look out expectantly from the frames. Not forgotten, neither can they forget.

And then there are the graves falling into ruin, the photos, faded and cracked, the images now faint shades of sepia. Are those men and women more than dead, now that even their names are nearly erased? Is the young man whose wreath is still fresh from the funeral, the flowers moist with dew or tears, still alive in comparison?

I cannot find Pasolini. I try again and retrace my steps, walking back up and down the rows under a sun heading into noon's high heat. He, no not he, I don't really believe that, not the man, but it, the grave, must be here. Must I go back to the hotel without finding it?

When I finally give up and start to leave, it's there on the right as I am about to exit the cemetery: two graves side by side,

> two flat white marble and matching
> stones. A tree grows out of the gravel,
> too small to shade them.

His mother, Susanna, is buried beside him. She was not told of her beloved son's death; she was told that he had gone on a long sea voyage.

•

The Pink House, 2004

On the main road leading from the train station to the piazza, the pink house. The stucco and paint were fresh; the building looked new, pristine though flanked by a vacant lot growing weeds and litter. The house had been his mother's home, not Pasolini's. As a boy Paolo came here during the summers for long visits, idyllic summers spent running with other boys, the golden-skinned, the sun-kissed sons of peasant farmers he came to love — all he would ever dream of desire. Later, during the war, when he was a university student at Bologna working on his thesis, he came here to get away from the bombing. At first he thought he hated it:

What a hell-hole this is after all. There's nothing here. It's dried-up, ugly, peopled by oafish men and shrewish women. The streets are gray dust and bare stones. Eight houses huddled together and called itself a town. And some fascist official listened and gave them the borough they deserved.

Was it really like this all along? Does my memory lie? Where are those green fields I loved as a boy? All year I would dream of returning here to run in the thigh-high grass, to fall again deliciously panting among the primroses, another boy beside me and everything free because everything was hidden by the long grass.

But now I see how shabby everything is, how small the square, how decrepit the houses. How the fields are dank, how the air is rank with the smell of decaying plants and stagnant waters. I came here again to get away from the war and found myself far from everything, on the very edge of existence.

This is the house where he stayed; this pink house was his mother's house. Here he wrote and self-published his first book of poetry, poems that he would write and rework for all his writing life.[1] But the house was bombed out during the war, reduced to charred rubble. Rebuilt, then neglected again when Pasolini, the young teacher, was fired for public indecency. And so the life in exile began. They left for Rome, Paolo and his mother. In his lifetime he

1 The poems written in Friulano and their many permutations published in 1975 as *La nuova gioventú*.

was reviled in the town, and he did not return again except in a coffin.

But now the pink house has been renovated, turned into a museum. Marco S., the director of the centre, was a few minutes late and apologized. It was unusual, this meeting to guide a single traveler. That morning he had led a tour, a group of 50 students from Udine.

•

All night I dreamt of his room; the desk facing the window, the light garish on the red and blue striped wall.

It is the morning of the second day and I return to *campo santo*. This time I know where he lies. I see the graves of his brother and the father he called the Colonel shielded by a fresco of angel warriors on the other, on the left as you leave the cemetery, where the right and the left have no more significance than to indicate direction.

Two sprigs of lavender for your grave,
scent of old woman's underwear
musky and sweet, a potpourri in my pocket

releases oily scent. Right for his mother
wrong for him. I should have
broken a branch from the cypress

lining the way to the cemetery,
their smell of green-spiced wood
more apt, more masculine.

(He seems to agree, flexing
his arm to show me the muscle)
Cypress is fiercer than flowers,

more potent than peppery poppies,
than honey-scented clover, or primrose,
or the wild yellow iris rising
from the ditches.

•

There are vineyards all around and in the fields behind the white stucco walls that enclose the cemetery. Such a haze today, blue grey, the horizon darkly smudged, the mountains (I know they're there, I saw them yesterday) totally obscured.

Old women, old men on their bicycles, make their way along the road to Valvasone, while the young drive by in cars or worse, raucous motor scooters. On a bench shaded by cypress, weeping for a man I have never met, I sit to write these notes and a voice whispers in Italian I don't know how to write.

Vado fuori dal paese e il cielo è scoperto,
Il mondo più grande che ho pensato,
Dove non c'è nessuno le stelle sono miliardo.

I jot the words down with the voice still sounding in my head. So much of what I'm writing is not writing at all, but dictation:

I leave the city and discover the sky,
The world is bigger than I realized,
Where there's nobody the stars are myriad.

II Impure Acts

How sweet is the shepherd's sweet lot!

(William Blake, *Songs of Innocence*)

I went to the Garden of Love,
And saw what I never had seen;
A Chapel was built in the midst,
Where I used to play on the green.

And the gates of this Chapel were shut,
And 'Thou shalt not' writ over the door;

(William Blake, *Songs of Experience*)

The Pink House, 1942

The house was painted pink and stood on a street leading from the railway station to the main square, one of two main streets. This square was the village's centre, if a village of eight houses can be said to have a centre. The village was called Casarsa della Delizia. Someone in the distant past and during a surely more prosperous time must have named it that, imagining the place to be a Garden of Eden. The land was flat and the soil was rich. The mountains in the distance to the north and east were the blue gates of this paradise. Rivers made the land fertile. The farmers grew grapes, and row on row of their golden green and trellised vines studded the landscape. They made grappa here, that distilled and potent essence of the grape. It was the only business and may have given the place the "delicious" part of its name. Casarsa was an ancient village and had survived many invasions, including the Turks who had burnt down all the original houses. Some thought that the fascists were the modern Turks; others were fascists themselves. Most of those who resisted took to the hills and joined the partisans. Those who stayed, if they resisted, resisted like water, when the Nazis stormed through them, they flowed around them.

Postscript(s)

The fall of '47 I was 25 and still living
in Viluta. What made me stay so long?
What made me linger in that nothing place,
        that hamlet of ten houses?

I remember November rain then more
rain flooding the courtyard, the sloshy silence
of a sodden Sunday night, all the world sopping,
        drip, dripping, except

for me, I am dry-eyed, I am a desert,
whatever the world is, I am not. The train
tracks beckoned me long ago when I was
        still a virgin I wanted

my body shattered, torn and rendered
the way it rendered me. Three years since first
I saw N. on the small bridge over the Vila,
        since first I heard the unbroken

crystal voice crying out to some unseen
friend, that lonesome calling an omen
of loss. Two and a half since that earthen
        hut where he succumbed

to my desire, one year since my love
for him began to wane as his body
waxed, limbs thickening, maturing, his mouth
        morphing into his mother's mouth.

So I felt no true sense of regret when
N. left town before me. The last time I heard
from him was in a letter to Mother, who taught
    him French, in a postscript

addressed to me: *je vous pense avec tendresse.*
Yet he bore all the weight of guilt, the leaden
burden of my sin. It's not for nothing
    these memories invade me

a quarter of a century later in the Eternal
City, in the wee hours when my desk lamp's
the only light on via Eufrate, the only light
    on the dark side of Earth.

It was the happiest, the saddest time in
my life, the glory of love, the horror
of war. The future was the past. Solely
    the present mattered: that slow

walk on the dark road to San Pietro,
the moon above us, a scimitar,
slipping into a grove of acacias to kiss
    unseen, safely to kiss.

War Smells Like Shit

Dark the hours when stars glitter in the obsidian
sky above, while on the horizon, the rising
moon spills milky light. I don't know if we'll
ever see each other again.

A day has passed; my youth has passed. All
day long I sat among abandoned vineyards,
in my body the wasteland of boredom.
Everything here smells

of endings, of shit and firing squads.
I haunted the unplowed fields, picked primroses
here and there, breathed in the green. The snowy
cap of mount Cavallo

seemed to float in the azure. Alone I
wandered the countryside, walking, walking,
walking the endlessly empty land. Everything
smells of gunpowder and shit

but the Earth's a bitch flowering anyway
from all that shit — in blossoms, blue and yellow,
in tender buds on the alders. I want
to spit farther than the farthest

mountains on the borders of our country
into the sea hidden behind them, I want to spit
into the faces of these villagers, these
Italians, these Christians.

Everything smells of firing squads and dirty feet —
(What keeps me tied to this blighted place? I must
stink myself.) I don't know if we'll ever
    see each other again.

The Return

Days were still cold though the light had lengthened.
Aquarius rising, the foothills faintly illuminated,
mystery on the far plain, we rode to it,
        returning in spring to our summers.

Tender memories of friendships, of solitudes,
all my clothes and books in a single suitcase,
we stepped off the night train and into morning,
        wearily walked the so familiar

street to Mother's ancestral house. I climbed
up to my old room to rest, marveling how
each year the timbers shrank and the room grew
        smaller. Noon became evening,

I woke to that crisp and candid air I knew
so well, to the smells of fire, of polenta,
of the iron pot, my grandmother stirring it.
        All around I heard breathing:

horses, humans, the whooshing wheels of bicycles.
Bells were calling us to vespers, voices
rose in prayer, in gossip, the incredible
    cadence of that tongue,

the open vowels, the sibilants, fricative,
strangely familiar inflections, flowering,
deflowering my ear. A feeling
        everywhere and inexpressible, filling

me with aching wonder at what I already
knew. There would be joys, triumphs, there would be
enormous losses and extraordinary consolations,
I could be — and I was — sure of it.

Bicycle Days

From early afternoon until dusk I would
ride my bicycle beyond the village
and into the distant plain. Turning on
        knees and spokes I became

one with the bicycle, propelled through sylvan
air, riding into the horizon, towards blue
mountains or the cloud embankments hiding
        them. Turning back at dusk, guided by

the yellow light of railroad tracks, in the damp
and sepulchral shadows, taking in the smells
of fire, of cooking, along with the calls,
        both raucous and sweet, to supper,

I would slow to watch some boy at a pump,
half-naked, sloughing off the dust of day —
I felt such thirst I could have lapped
        the run-off from his body —

or another, sitting back on a doorstep
with angelic indifference to bathing,
indifferent too to my eyes on his bare limbs,
        his sinews shining as if oiled

in the glow of a darkening world, as I, vile
and guilty worshiper not worthy of even
a glance, passed by furtively towards home,
        towards the sadly ringing bells.

La Bella Stagione

Those were blue-sky days. We took our lessons
outdoors, in the sun, sitting on the front steps
reciting Dante to peach and almond trees
        in the beautiful season,

late March, their pink and white blossoms vibrant
against the faint, the hallucinatory green
of new leaf. It all seemed so perfect,
        the bombs might have been petals

dropping thickly from above. Untouched we
watched the panorama of smoke rising in
pinnacles, massifs on the near horizon, but then,
        barely a kilometre away,

the train station blew up. I did not take up a gun
like my brother. I did not die for our freedom.
I took up the pen, arming boys too young to fight
        with words, not bullets.

The Bombers

First the alarm sounded in nearby Castiglione.
Looking to the horizon the fields were
dazzlingly dark. Clouds rose in marble columns
then the tender turquoise of sky split.

Like distant thunder the first rumblings of planes
— some reconnaissance craft. Throbbing engines
coming closer and closer, a squadron of bombers
obliterating sleep,

the sweet silence of farm and village at dawn.
Silver blades ploughed through air, in their wake
a vapour trail. They flew in a mathematical
line towards railway tracks,

towards factories, towards Venezia
or Bavaria. Just imagining it blew
the stink of blood and burning that rose from
the wreckage our way.

Women kept at their chores while boys who watched
shouted the number, direction, altitude
of the planes, their size, their nation, as if
facts — mere figures — could protect us.

Bombs dropped on the bridge over the Tagliamento,
bombs exploded in Castiglione. Ear-
splitting. Then the cold relief of the blasts
thinning out in the distance.

Angels of death had passed over our homes
as if innocent blood, our neighbours', were
painted on our doors; we were spared because
          others suffered.

Night of the Merry-go-round

(Vieni, c'è una strada nel bosco)

That night a gramophone was playing: *come*
there's a path through the woods.... Under an orange
moon, the merry-go-round kept on turning.
I remember the song and the scent

of wisteria and linden. I felt an
orgy of emotion, tears I dared not
let fall for a boy on the bridge, body
against the railing, plaintively

calling to some unseen companion, and not
to me. I was with my soccer buddies
when I first met B. He was a boy without
real beauty. Though there were glimmers

of violet light in his black eyes, his coarseness
filled me with loathing: his lower lip, scarred,
his neck thick, his undershirt soiled, a torso
sun-burned and smelling

of dust, of stale cigarettes and river water.
In front of us all, shamelessly he urinated
against a tree. He walked with the padding
steps of a predator. Still I

paid for his rides on the merry-go-round.
Still I rode with him into the night. I don't
recall how it all ended. If I walked
home with him, or alone. But

I remember . . . *a path through the woods . . .*
playing over and over, the orange moon
smelling of flowers, the bridge, and the lonesome
boy there, his plaintive calling.

Devil Among the Angels

The church seemed vacant, only a few shadows
cast without bodies kneeling here and there
in the pews. Some votive candles flickered
        and smoked. The floor oozed a vernal

dampness, smelling of earthworms and new grass.
At the back, by the fountain of holy
water I stood mouthing *mea culpa,*
        mea culpa, mea culpa . . .

that litany to which, little by little,
I had become stone-deaf. The altar boys
in their long robes bowed as if with the weight
        of wings, the scraped and sun-burnished

knees I knew so well hidden away, lost
in the folds of their cassocks. Ceintures
of purple silk rope hung from their slim waists.
        One boy held out the missal

for the priest to read. His stance, his gesture,
was moving but distressing too as if
I were watching a scene from ancient Greek
        theatre where I played the roles

of son, king and murderer. After Mass
the boys flew out the back door, joyous
to be free, playing a game designed just,
        or so it seemed, to torture me:

lighting long matches made of clear mica
they would throw them into the air setting
the night on fire, the darkness streaked with such
          a luminous downpour of torches.

At the Gravel Pit/Without a Word

The gravel pit was behind the cemetery.
Afternoons, the sons of labourers and farmers
would swim there in the pond, most of them
        naked, even the older boys.

After lunch I would go there, heart racing
with the wheels of my bicycle, I went
not to swim, but to read books in the sun,
        useless when B. would enter

the scene smoking the end of a cigarette.
Without looking at me, without a word
he'd strip down for a dip. My passion
        for him was paralyzing.

The young boys were sexless as sparrows, no
more exciting to watch than babies in
a bath, but B. was a satyr, his bird
        rivaled Priapus.

Ragged clothes piled on burlap sacks he stretched
out on the bank beside me, his wet body,
lead turned into gleaming gold, alchemy
        of sunlight on water.

Without a word we would move into the maize
nearby where, shielded from the sun's eye, where,
shielded from all eyes, we would masturbate
        together. Did I love him? Not

if that's the same word a poet might use,
that Petrarch used for Laura, or Dante
for Beatrice, no, it was not the same
word as I used for N.

At Your Service

After the hour of splendour in the corn field
I would help B. gather grasses to feed
his rabbits and after the sacks were filled
        I would walk him home.

He could not have imagined that behind
my reserve, my barely-able-to-speak
mouth, that behind the so-polite manner,
        was hidden such emotion, such

ecstasy from my first taste of physical
love. He could not have imagined (though surely
he felt it) that I was in his power,
        that I was at his service.

My First Date

I

No one who lives a normal life can
imagine what a miracle it seems
getting the first date; it was God-given,
        that glorious day in late spring.

The grass was drunk on sunlight, the first birds
trilling, the mulberry trees fully unfurling
lush leaves. I left for my date not daring
        to believe in it. Stealthily

I went down the dripping underground way
by the embankment, afraid I might be
seen, afraid of all the suppositions,
        the gossip that might follow me.

No glancing over my shoulder. I did
not want to turn back. The closer I came,
the less I expected to reach the unreachable,
        to realize the unrealizable.

II

There was no sign of sheep or of their keeper,
no B. Solitude must be my destiny.
I heard the woo-woo-woo of a whistle,
        the crew's shouts. As a train

chugged into the station I could smell the stink
of latrines, the reek of excrement leaking
onto the tracks, and so sank my hopes for
    a life not alone. The first sheep

appeared, and then came B., wearing coarse
baggy trousers, huge clogs on his feet, but
naked to the waist. With that uneven gait
    and sun-burned unlovable face

he came to my side. He let me squeeze his
arm, then his thigh. On the dry yet still damp
river bed we ambled deliciously
    complicit into the thickets.

B. worried about secrecy even
more than I did and could find such deeply
hidden spots — the better concealed, the more
    open his lust.

But B. was never in much of a hurry
for love. He climbed a tree, snatched a nest
full of eggs, and pushing holes in the tops
    drank them all down

then he rolled one of his foul cigarettes
and smoked. I can see the scene, replayed in
slow motion with a soundtrack of outraged
    birds, moving into darker woods.

III

My first date was not all I hoped for, not
the first in a series. B. was fickle, B. was
rascally, often he found reasons for us
        not to meet. Every day

I walked and rewalked the dirt road to B.'s
village, scouring the path by the embankment,
if I found sheep droppings they seemed triumphant
        signs of his presence, his passing.

For ten days, and many times a day, I
went searching along the path. He must be
out there somewhere nearby; B. was absent
        in a teasing, visible way.

In desolation I whiled away hour after
hour to whistles, to rumblings of trains
and the vague, the vilest odour of feces,
        in fervent grumblings, in jealousies.

Spring Far Behind

Winter came and our days at the pond, long
days of lazing and love, were gone. With no
excuse to meet, looking for B. became
        my real, my only occupation.

He was growing up and that made me jealous,
made me gloomy. Our couplings I knew were
trifling. He erected invisible walls
        against me. I pined for his

insouciant body, I suffered his
indifference to my love, that male callousness.
How could he pass my house without a sign,
        without a soupçon

of feeling? As if he didn't know me! While
I would have given everything I had
just for a glance, a knowing glance, a nod,
        a wink my way. In that winter

of deprivation, of despair, I dreamed of spring,
of meeting the boy flagrantly skipping school,
of lying with him in a familiar bed,
        some ditch fragrant with primrose.

Hidden Corners/The Earth Moves

The new green in spring is acid yellow,
the first birds sing a medley of chirps and
whistles, the mulberry trees open their leaves
        like hands to receive

the benediction of rain, of sunlight.
O there was no sin if there was no B.!
I heard human voices, I listened for
        words in the singing of birds.

Infinity was waiting. When at last he came,
he came naked to the waist! He led
while I followed, close as his noon shadow
        into some hidden corner of woods.

The dew had dried but the stones, gravel
from the river bank, still glistened; in the grove
where we lay together the Earth trembled
        with the passing trains.

A Thousand Birds

Summer again and that drama I played
such a mortifying role in changed. We
went back to swimming at the pit, back to
        the hullabaloo of boys.

I saw B. there every day though he rarely
heeded my come-hither looks. I frittered
away hours, seated with books, my Tasso,
        my Tommaseo, a thousand

birds sang in different scales, alternating
then harmonizing. Sweetly they let silence,
now modulated by human voices,
        by trills and shrills,

absolutely animal fill me. Every
thing distracted, yet stoked my obsession,
my envy for those meadows where B. stepped
        shoeless into the long grass.

Hide-and-Go-Seek

B. was already naked and I saw,
with such quivering joy, or I imagined,
he too was eager for me to untie
        the knot of my swimsuit.

When playing hide-and-go-seek with the boys
I naturally chose the same hiding place
as B. But for days he would just vanish
        and I went crazy, jealous

for the places that saw him, for the grass
crushed by his naked feet. When he came back
to the pit, he would, with condescension,
        leering, lure me into the maize.

I don't believe — and it's not to absolve myself
of guilt that I say this — I don't believe
I was the player; no, coldly, without
        a doubt, he made me follow him.

The G. Period

Pan across the courtyard and garden at Ilde's:
chicken coop and hog pen stand to the left
of the house. Tilt up to the second floor,
to that room above the kitchen

where the nascent director, lingering in bed,
looks to the window, picturing the scenario
below. Now tilt back down to the courtyard.
Track G. in his hunter trousers

and Bolero jacket, pacing as he talks
on an equal footing with the elders, not
sparing them from his irony or his
little laughs. Zoom

in on the boy's face, downy cheeks, tender
lips, small miracles. His hands are hidden
in his pockets, his smile flirts between boy
wonder and know-it-all. Zoom

out to the glistening trellis, the flowering
vines in dappled light one autumn afternoon
in '44, rolling on a loop in my dream,
flickering on its silver screen.

The G. Period: The Soundtrack

The prattle from the kitchen below could
be the rattling of gravel thrown against
the window. Could be confetti shattering
    on the ceramic floor.

Could be a rain of hail and petals. Cutlery
jangles in a drawer brusquely opened, then
slammed shut. Dawn's trumpeting of light, rooster
    let loose among the hens.

Scent of cyclamen, a crimson aria. Wind
in the trees, murmurings. Then something draws
the boy outside. Lightly scuffling clogs cross
    the stone courtyard. Dead air.

The gate, a creak, then a clank. Buoyant steps
running off, fading towards some point far from
the director's ear, beyond the recording,
    and (almost) beyond his imagining.

Colour on Sunday

Nothing could lessen that human desire
to celebrate. Sirens might sound, bombers
might darken the sky, but nothing could stop
        us from donning our Sunday best

and strolling together to Mass. Courtyards
swept Saturday night, not a fleck of straw
left behind, sparkled. Sun shimmered on roofs
        in blessing. Colours

were richer, more intense. Boys in short pants
with thick woolen knee socks and bright blazers
flocked like tropical birds. G. in blue, his
        suit with the white collar!

In my burgundy jersey, hair combed, shoes buffed,
I was all dressed up too and, heart flapping,
joined the procession to the cathedral.
        On Mondays, Tuesdays,

other days, the verdant fields were no longer
all bathed in a zinc luster, they seemed flat,
merely painted, fixed as in a masterpiece,
        all art, not life.

Sunday Dinner/Olympic Games

At a small table, in our makeshift home,
alone, Mother and I would dine in silence,
preserving a porcelain-and-silver decorum,
        sombre, sober, solemn,

while below us G.'s whole clan feasted.
They shouted, they declaimed, embroiled in raucous
ongoing fighting amongst themselves.
        Their meals were Olympic games.

They did not sit together or share the same
food. The youngest children could not be coaxed
to eat, they stood up on their chairs and scolded
        their elders. First course was soup,

yellow with fat, but thin on pasta. The men,
labourers who knew no rest, ate squatting
by the fire, cradling bowls, coarse and white
        like calcified hands.

Birthday Poem

It was the fifth of March, my birthday, but
joyless for me and Mother who missed her
other son, Guido, the one fighting in
        la Resistenza, dead barely

a month though neither of us knew it then.
The day, serene, the blue heralding the end
of war, the blossoming of hope. Mother and
        I slept in the same room,

our only room, in beds that by day served
as sofas. Soon birds would come to the window
facing the mountains where Guido hid, bringing
        (Mother believed) good news of him.

After Dinner Story

G.'s father was a natural philosopher.
All would gather round to listen to him.
One story lingers in my mind as does
        that long ago night sitting under

summer stars. Something was filmy, fragile
in the tale, something barely articulated,
too hard to repeat, too hard to forget.
        He spoke to an owl's hooting —

Somewhere over the moonlit fields . . . who knows
when, what night in my youth, I was travelling
in a wagon, who knows where, I cannot
        remember anything but this,

a wren or titmouse followed me chittering
in a language it seemed I half understood,
at times circling, at times preceding, leading
        me into the deepening dusk . . .

Birthday Dream

That night we went to sleep much less depressed
than usual. O the smell of spring promised
mending, promised the end of the
        endless bombings. We slept soundly

until Ilde woke us all. In the blackout
she had seen a gleam of light in the field.
We hoped that the planes flying over us
        endlessly at night had not seen

it. The only other light was in the sky,
the glint of steely stars. All was silent,
tranquil, the only sounds, sounds of sleeping,
        pigs snuffling in their pens,

the breath of a breeze joined by sighs of relief
that it was not an unexploded bomb —
but a plough, the blade blinking in starlight.
        We dragged it back into the barn

then, too fearful to sleep, huddled together
there for an hour, the women whispering,
knitting by candlelight, the men smoking,
        the children glad to trade in

dreams for marbles. Nobody laughed at Ilde's
fears, at the light that might have marked us,
might yet draw the bombers back, calling down
        on us a rain of fire.

Birthday Nightmare

The second birth, they say, is the harder.
Again that night my mother and I woke,
this time shaken from our beds by the same
        deafening dream, the rumble, the roar

of planes as through the roof a charred branch crashed
onto the dresser. The whole house shook, lurched
to one side; it seemed to groan then fall on
        one knee. In the chaos

of overturned furniture, choking on
plaster dust and smoke we had to crawl to
each other. Sky gaped through the red-tiled roof,
        now the north wall was all window,

mountains appeared etched on the horizon.
Down crumbling stairs we fled our second home.
It was dawn by then, our town turned into
        a towering field of flame,

a panorama of orange and yellow smoke.
Huddled outside we watched the conflagration,
all that stood between us and that inferno
        now in high relief,

in vegetal sentience, unperturbed:
the trees loaded with buds, the geraniums
in clay pots, the delicate trellis-work
        of vines, and the dung heap.

The Dream's Aftermath

That morning was clear and cold, the fire
burning up the town did not warm us
as we loaded carts, salvaging what we could
　　　of our household goods, G. helping,

G. getting underfoot, telling the adults
what to do, his tongue sniping as sharply
as ever, G., cheeks flushed, the house destroyed
　　　was just an adventure for him.

He was leaving but wouldn't even look at
me. No nod to what we were. Their cart was
heaped with sacks of stuff, mattresses, and G.
　　　perched himself on top, laughing.

I said goodbye, all my sadness had to be
implied. But he was eager to be off,
as if all memory of home, school and (O)
　　　my love had been erased.

Red Rags Where My Heart Used to Be

Winter seemed to return the day we left
our home of two years for Valuta.
The sky was blanched, the countryside muddy
    and bare. In ploughed fields, water

brimmed, furrows forming long canals, under
dark, bloated clouds lay an expanse of ruin,
the smell of smoldering coal, the smell of charred
    bodies stoking our fears.

Our wagon had to go around huge mounds
of debris blocking the roads. In this wreckage
of a land, in this land of wreckage there was
    no one. The groaning wheels echoed

from the deep craters left by bombs as if
the sound of pain were the only sign of life.
In the rubble that had once been homes, here
    and there from twisted beams and

crumbled walls hung red flags, really just rags,
sagging with rain, warning against sleeping
bombs. Three marked our house, less fit to live in
    without G. than without walls.

We had worked all day, loading the wagon
with stuff that could be salvaged. N. helping,
impressed by our middle-class things, a silk
    pillow, a rare vase — he enjoyed

the work so I enjoyed it too. Now he
was walking beside me behind the cart,
his shirt was drenched with rain and sweat, his
        trousers mud-splattered, his dark

curls matted, and this made him all the more
desirable to me. G. was gone. Even
though I had N. nearby, constant, caring,
        hanging on my every word,

the boy was not then truly mine. In my
reckless, unruly — in my O so stubborn
heart, without the sex the world calls vice, no
        other love for me could suffice.

Soul and Body

She combed my hair, plucked a flower and put
it behind my ear — Pina, my companion,
my soulmate, Pina, who just had to know
    my every thought, my every tic,

who must leave nothing hidden between us,
except what she must not know, except what
I could tell no one. We were lying in
    the sacred solitude of the fields,

she, dying of desire and I dying
of boredom, desiring only the sun-bronzed
B., picturing him wearing Turkish trousers
    and white silk socks.

Lessons in Latin

Late March sun, raw, renewed, dazzles the stone
of the courtyard and cobbles of the road.
Time to throw open windows, to inhale
        sunlight, its scent of hay

in the hayloft, to breathe in the odour
of cedar as the balcony's wood recalls
the tree it once was. A whiff of silk, my
        bedspread daydreaming mulberry,

the worm's memory in its weave. A sun so
resplendent we could take the musty books,
our Latin lessons, down to the river,
        where it curves, *amo, amas,*

amat, amus. . . . Poplars teeming with buds,
their branches arabesque the sky. Primroses
underfoot echo sun. And N. reading
        aloud, poetry in the rough,

his first verses in dialect, tough music,
music with heft, broad-shouldered. Gutturals
astound me, the sound of his words entering,
        rolling in my ear, their purr, not

their purpose. The reading's stopped now and then
by the flight of some bird N. names for me:
cuckoo, oriole, wren — O their songs need
        no primers, no prosodies.

My False Faith

My first doubt came with my first real sin
though I longed for a simple faith, I longed
to be oblivious as a boy playing
        ball in a sunlit field.

Stepping from bright sunlight into the dark
dank church I could not see, I could only
smell wet plaster and the pungent cedar
        timbers. I knelt at the feet

of the statue of the Madonna, her robe
dipped in the molten blue of the serene
sky I left behind to plead for forgiveness,
        to pray to change, to pray

to be like other men — upstanding — not
to hide watching, different and desiring.
After a hundred Hail Marys I could
        hear her breathing. She seemed

to sway, her arms outstretched, not to embrace,
but for balancing, her first toddling steps were
to be made for me. Still she came no closer;
        painted pink, her lips did

not part, did not speak, and I felt bereft,
left with a keen nostalgia for the Divine
that would never again be mine. There were
        sins I dare not divulge

to this day. I prayed for N. dying in
his narrow bed, brow burning with fever,
a glistening moustache of sweat where no hair
        had yet to darken his upper lip.

His pending death had to be a punishment.
I prayed that it be mine, not his. I promised
not to touch him again if only Heaven
        would spare the boy! These

confessions, these false promises, I wrote
in Greek in the margins of my notebook
so that no one could read them. I offered
        my life instead, but my mother

still grieved for Guido and I was her last,
her only son while N.'s mother had four
other boys. Thus went my puerile prayers,
        my petty bargaining with the Virgin.

The next day with N. fully recovered
from the sniffles fear had inflated
into pneumonia, I could not escape
        my plague, nor resist the dark

rose of his budding body, I kept
breaking anew my vows not to touch
the boy sacrificing his innocence
        to my lewd caresses.

E Se Fosse Vero?

Pina's sister was the first to guess
my love for one of my students was
something else, something that threatened her own.
        And if it were true?

Music was our damper for the danger,
evenings Pina and I would play duets,
it mattered not at all if we were drowned
        out by the thundering drone

of night raiders flying above, dropping
more bombs. We kept playing music unheard
even over our own wildly drumming
        hearts. In the conflagration,

our concert, a mime. After the bombers
had gone, we packed up our flutes and I would
walk her home, not to her door, but stopping
        at the gate as I was afraid of her

dogs, but then she would insist on walking
me back. In spite of my protests this farce
went on, back and forth, until we parted
        halfway. There she reached for my face —

was it to kiss my lips? I turned away
and she kissed the air, the crystalline fog
of my breath. *And if it were true* that I
        loved her not, that I loved

a boy more, what then were these hours shared
while the village slept the sleep of the soon
to be dead? Light in the darkness: the moon
    glittering on whitened, glassy fields.

Already Old

"Fourteen! I'm already old," said my true
love, N., though still playing with his friends
after church, kicking a ball made of rags
        every which way. On the church's

neat linen of lawn, the boys played soccer,
running, shouting, N., the bell of his voice
beginning to crack. I was 20, but
        seemed much younger. For 10,

12, for umpteen Sundays when the sun shone
and the wings darkening the sky above us
were few, I played ball with the boys for hours
        not pausing until the azure

heavens turned indigo. Those blazing blue
days were divine unless the bombers came
back, then we ran for cover as those angels
        of death swept over us.

All That Sparkles

As the house faced south, all day long it basked
in the sun. From the balcony I could see:
the clothesline below sagging with laundry,
        the courtyard, its trellis

of vines and vases of flowers in olive,
in sylvan light, and the horizon where mountains
seemed sculpted in blue marble. That morning
        everything sparkled.

Sparkle, what a vital and knotty sense
that verb held for me then. From the mountains
down to the great plain, from the fields of Castiglione
        to the poplars by the Vila,

the river bordering on F.'s land — everything
sparkled. The orchard bloomed in pink and white,
the blossoms looked like a swarm of butterflies
        shot in stop-motion.

The peach and almond trees stood out starkly
against the acid green of new grain as if
made of wax, a pale blond and rosy wax
        under the whitewashing sun.

My love for N. filled my chest. I could breathe
in, not out. Books by my side, pen in hand,
the blank page would fill with his likeness. As
        the sky began to bleed I would

visualize him leaning against a pillar
of the portico, resting at last, somewhat
bored listening to the hammering of horseshoes
        on the anvil, a farmer's

evensong. His figure in twilight troubled
with shadow, taking on mystery, enthralled
me. But likely N. never allowed himself
        such moments of indolence.

Still out of the darkroom of my mind
a picture emerged of a body wholly
anonymous, a young hero, Jason
        donning the Golden Fleece.

More likely N. rushed to eat, rushed to finish
his last chores, rushed with books to our house
where I waited for him, crazy with impatience.
        He would appear at the turn

in the road, running towards me, clutching his
books, but, mesmerized by the mythic,
that amorphous image I had formed of him,
        I failed to see the boy.

To the Nightingale Singing in the Elder Grove in the Summer of '44

Teach me music, teach me your way
with adagio, allegretto, con brio. . . .

You, your solo without the violin, your chamber
an elder grove in the summer,

on this August night unnamable
notes — your song

full of stops, 20 tempos
(all short

then the longest rests). How might I sing
(in even one)

that measured, that slowly heart-rending
air with more descant

than discord as I am torn
and out of tune.

The Same Moon

The moon looks like a wad of bloody rags,
            she said. We had
walked beyond the village lights and lingered

            listening to silence.
That moon, I said, used to shine
            on Sappho's shoulders,

my throat thick with yesterday's tears and something
            untouchable
completely outside of us.

Dancing After the War

I

The sky is all mist, grey and amethyst.
Sunday mutes the courtyard, stables, manure
pits in gilded, in glistening silence, a dream
        where birds must swim or drown

in air. Mother has gone to weep at Guido's
grave. It's fate that I'm alone in our small
rented room where I watch as if dreaming:
        the white plaster ceiling,

the black tiles, my desk, a table littered
with books, papers, the red sofa serving
as my bed where N. and I sometimes stretched
        out. I waited and I am still

waiting for N. and the other boys to call
to my window or climb the wood staircase
smelling of bleach up to my room. The boys
        are at ease with me

outside the classroom, they trust the dancer
more than the teacher. N. wears the silk shirt
that I gave him, its maroon a smoldering
        mirror where I lose myself.

I will wake up still drunk to a morning
spectacular, to a life that's spectacular.
I love N., I love the boys and this village,
        Viluta, above all cities.

II

When the war ended, the dancing began.
At every Saint's feast, from villages all
around the region, boys congregated,
        I can still see them

the dark, gangling boys from Valvasone;
the boys from Alta, voices, faintly foreign,
their dialect from before the railroad;
        the blond boys from San Pietro

where blond is a gritty gold, agile yet
hefty as horses; the stylish from San Quirino
with their urbane talk, their Venetian tones,
        ironic, insolent bucks

and from Bassa came the greenest of all
the boys, bumpkins with their shoes tied around
their necks, Sunday-best jackets straining at
        the seams, hands crammed into pockets.

The dance hall was an extended waiting
room, its sides were lined with benches where boys
sat suddenly shame-faced. At the far back
        a bar sold the wine of their

fathers. We danced the boogie woogie, we
shimmied and shook, but shuffled with the slow
songs, we, the boys from Viluta, dancing
        alone, dancing together.

III

Sonorous air. Winter, spring, boys, young men
flocking together on bicycles, birds
on wheels. Going to, going home from the
        dance, nights on empty

wind-swept streets, the local boys on foot,
breaking into boogie woogies, singing
drunkenly "When the roo-oo-ster crows . . ."
        Stars fading fast

as Sunday becomes Monday. Stopping at M.'s
house to eat cold polenta, salami,
and drink more wine. Birds, everything, everyone
        singing, singing full-throated

singing through the sleeping streets, trumpeting
"when the rooster crows . . . when the roo-oo-oo . . ."
holding hands, N. hovering by my side
        always in the almost morning.

June 2, 1946

All day rain falls as if it were autumn.
Though I cannot go to the dance I feel
almost lighthearted, I feel almost gay
    in my bottomless boredom —

I feel, oh my love, as if new born. Voices
rise from the courtyard, voices that muted
in drumming rain sound distant as the stars,
    as the heavens where,

though hidden, I know they still glimmer. As
if it were autumn rain falls and all day
in my mind images of you, your face,
    come into view, unbidden,

forbidden. Why does remembering make them
dimmer? Like the cloud-covered sky, your lips,
when you smile to yourself, part as beams of
    sunlight breaking through.

When I Was Good, Still

It was a time when I was good to all
the world, a time when all the world still called
me good. The smoke from Ilde's kitchen mounts
        in my memory, the farmyard is

frosted over, the air, crystal, the river
embroidered with ice. I can still smell burnt
straw and dunghills and see the flurry of birds
        gusting from F.'s hedges —

see in the near dark the chapel haloed
in pink, the fields flat, beaten steel, shining —
the sickle moon, hoisted on the horizon,
        blue mountains, their crests smudged

with crimson, the shades of sunset unstaunched,
as the light dims the glow from small yellow
lamps deepening, in my mind these images
        emerge in montage.

Everything found its sense, its eloquence
in the rose, in the blush of N.'s cheeks. N.,
head on my shoulder, N. shy, modest, still
        smelling of milk, N. revering

my every word . . . and so, in spite of
the bombings, in spite of the war it was
the fullest time in my life, it persists,
        the life within my life.

III

After Pasolini

The dead are not
silent we are
deaf to them.

(after Pasolini)

'44–49 The Day of My Death

In some city, Trieste or Udine,
    on an avenue of lindens,
in the spring, when leaves
    burst into colour,
    I'll fall
under a sun that blazes
        yellow and high
    and I will close my eyes
    leaving the sky to its splendour.

Under a linden, warm with green,
    I will fall into the darkness
of my death, a death that squanders
    the lindens, the sun.
    Beautiful boys
flying out from school,
        curls at their temples.
    will be running in that light
    I have only just lost.

I will be young still,
    in a pastel shirt
and with soft hair spilling
    into the bitter dirt.
    I will be warm still
and a boy running on the warm
        asphalt of the avenue
    will lay a hand
    on the crystal of my lap.

'74 The Day of My Death

. . . if the seed of grain, fallen on the earth, does not die,
it remains alone, but if it dies it gives great fruit.

John 12:24 (cited by Dostoevsky)

In some city, Trieste or Udine,
        on an avenue of lindens,
when leaves changed colour . . .
        he lived
with the vigour of a young man,
            in the midst of things,
        and he gave, to the few
        men he knew, everything.

Then, for the love of those boys
        with curls at their foreheads
boys like him until just before
        the stars overhead
        altered their light —
he would have liked to give his life
        for the world of strangers,
himself, a stranger, a little saint,
a solitary seed lost in the sand.

But instead he wrote
        sacred poetry
believing that way
        his heart would flourish.
        Days went by
in a labour that used
        up the grace in his heart:
the seed did not perish,
and he remained alone.

The Day of His Death, November 1, 1975

. . . if the seed of grain, fallen on the earth, does not die, it remains alone, but if it dies it gives great fruit.

John 12:24

In some city, not after all
        Trieste or Udine, but in Rome,
though not on its streets of ancient stone
        but on the margins, in shantytown —
not in spring, on some avenue of flowering
        yellow linden, but golden in autumn,
with the first cold rain, with the leaves he falls
        the sun well past its gloaming
in the no light of night alone.

For the love of boys, or for the love of one lost
        boy with curls darkening his brow,
a beautiful boy, a frog prince, he would give his last
        lira for the love of this or any stranger
to whom he owes nothing, or all, a bit of money, a hot
        meal, an embrace with no backward
looking goodbye. In blue jeans, his shirt now blood-
        soaked, his body cooling, his body cooler
        than the sand under his shoes, sand

warm when he was still warm moments
        before and forever
closed his eyes under blinking stars,
a man not yet old, a man not
        a saint, but with a saint's
love for strangers, lying face up in the dirt,
        on a feast day, on All Saints' at last
a seed squandered no longer
        beaten on the beaten ground of Ostia.

IV Epilogue:
The Book

I. Prologue: The Flower and the Book

When, in the spring of 2004, I visited Pasolini's grave in Casarsa, he whispered a few lines of verse to me. Although I poorly transcribed them as I cannot write in Italian and my ear filtered the words through the *abruzzese* dialect, my first language, I have corrected the errors in spelling and grammar with the help of Anna Foschi. Clearly no miracle occurred; clearly what I heard was totally imagined, but imagined through poetry. That is the way the muse spoke to me on that day.

Home again in Canada I woke up one morning dreaming of the pink house.

The pink house was his mother's ancestral home; it was bombed out during the war and had to be rebuilt; he never lived in it again. But the region, Friuli, its dialect, the war, his homosexuality, formed the historical and personal vortex that shaped his identity, his political ideas, and all his creative work. I imagined I would write a novel based on what I had read in biographies and histories about Pasolini and those war years. But when I read the original source about his life, his own memoir of the period, what emerged was not a war story, but a coming-of-age one, a kind of gay *Sorrows of Young Werther*. It really surprised me how little the war figures in the narrative; the big war, World War II, is marginalized by the virtual war inside him between the moral imperatives established by church, community, and family and his sexual desire for boys. The coming-of-age story is the coming into difference. The bombings formed a mere backdrop to his tortured struggles with his sexuality.

II. Impure Acts

The poems in this section, which make up the core of this book, are based on that memoir of his youth and the war years, *Atti impuri*, published in 1982, nearly a decade after his death. It was published in conjunction with the autobiographical novel or novella based on this period of his life, *Amado Mio*, whose protagonist is an allegorically named self, Desiderio. The same material, the same experience, but through thinly disguised third person narration.

My poems, this book, form a kind of novel in verse based on the experiences, feelings, Pasolini describes in the memoir. I do not judge him, he judges himself; when he is not rationalizing he sees his desire as sin, himself as the devil. When I first approached this material, I imagined writing the story perhaps from the point of view of his female friend at the time, Pina. But the sense of time I kept encountering in the memoir was that of poetry, not prose. The narrative seemed concentrated in the sense of the moment, circling around and around a few spots in time without the sense of progression characteristic of the novel; a lyrical sense of time: compressed, recurring, suspended, essential, *eternity in an hour.*

III. After Pasolini

The book that launched Pier Paolo Pasolini as a writer was *La Meglio Gioventú. The Flower of Youth*, usually translated as *The Best of Youth*, was a volume of verse written in dialect and self-published in 1942. That he should choose to begin his writing career by publishing poetry, in a time of war, in a minority tongue, poems about peasant life, might seem an anomalous beginning for such a polemical writer, a writer who spent his entire life at the centre of political thought and culture in Italy. That he should continue to work on these poems throughout his life speaks to their centrality to his poetic project. Published in 1975, the year of his death, *La Nuova Gioventú, The New Youth,* is comprised of those original poems written in dialect during the war and the many permutations on them that he called the second form of *La Meglio Gioventú.*

These were the first and last poems that Pasolini wrote, pastoral poems written in a time of war, when his region was occupied by the Germans, and Mussolini, then a puppet leader, had been set up in Salò. His younger brother, Guido, took up arms and fought with the resistance while Pier Paolo took up the pen; along with his mother he set up a school to teach boys too young to go to war and began to write poetry in dialect. To write poems in dialect in a country where the ministry of culture outlawed the use of dialects was a form of resistance in itself.

But what can music do

Against the weapons of soldiers?

In Virgil's *Eclogues* the iron age of war intrudes on the idyllic life of singing shepherds; that is the convention of the pastoral. This seemed an apt epigraph. My translation of the lines is assisted by David Ferry's.

Although I have only encountered references to Pasolini having read Wordsworth, Blake seemed to me the poet with the closest parallel to what he does with his different versions of the Casarsa poems. However, Blake's *Songs of Innocence* and *Songs of Experience* are separated by one year while Pasolini's encompass the whole of his writing life. I translated *La Meglio Gioventú* for myself as a preparation to write this book, translation being, I believe, the closest a writer can come to another writer, but only my translations of his "The Day of My Death" are included here. I close my book with that poem in which Pasolini envisions his death, the first version written during the war years, the permutation on it published in the year of his death; my permutation on them is based on the reported circumstances of his actual death in Rome on All Saints' Day, November 1, 1975.

Sources

Naldini, Nico. *Pasolini, una vita*. Einaudi Editore, 1989.

Pasolini, Pier Paolo. *Amado Mio*. Garzanti, 2000.

——. *La Nuova Gioventu, Poesie friulane 1941–1974*. Einaudi Editore, 1975.

——. *poesie*. Garzanti, 1970.

Schwartz, Barth David. *Pasolini Requiem*. Pantheon Books, 1992.

Virgil. *Eclogues*. Translated by David Ferry. Farrar, Straus, and Giroux, 1999.

Acknowledgements

Early drafts of some of these poems first appeared in *Branch*, *CVII*, *jacket*, *Drunken Boat*, *Event*, *Matrix*, *The Malahat Review*, *Poetry Quebec*, *Rhythm*, and on the Parliamentary Poet Laureate of Canada website.

I would like to thank Roo Borson and Kim Maltman, my first readers of the manuscript for their comments and encouragement. I would also like to thank Concordia University for an internal grant that helped me with the travel and research costs for this book. Special thanks to Gianni Scalia of the University of Bologna, a friend of Pasolini, who not only shared his memories of the man, but also gave me his personal and annotated copy of Nico Naldini's *Pasolini, una vita*.

Thank you Michael Holmes for believing in this book, and Tania Craan for her wonderful work on the cover image.